THE HIST

50 EVENTS

BY

Stephan Weaver

© 2015 Copyright

TABLE OF CONTENTS

Prehistoric India

Vedic India

The Rule of the Aryans—1500 BC

The Most Ancient Hindu Scriptures - The Vedas - are Penned—1500-1100 BC

The Upanishads—the Foundations of Hinduism—are Written—800-500 BC

Buddhism is Founded 500 BC—500 BC

Jainism is Founded 500 BC—600 BC

The Persian Conquest (Achaemenid Rule) —530 (538) BC

India Under Great Empires

Alexander the Great Conquers India—326 BC

The Mauryan Empire is Established—322 BC

The Kushan Empire is Established—30 BC

The Gupta Empire Begins (The Golden Age of India)
—320-550 AD

India is Conquered by Muslims—712 AD

The Delhi Sultanate—1206-1526 AD

16ᵗʰ Century India

The First European Settlement in India—1503

Battle of Diu—1509

Establishment of Portuguese India—1510

Rise of the Mughal Empire—1526

Akbar the Great, Emperor of the Mughal Empire—

1556

17th Century India

Formation of the East India Company—1600-1612

British India—1612

French India—1642

Completion of the Taj Mahal—1653

Establishment of the Maratha Empire—1674

Danish India—1620

18th Century India

Battle of Plassey—1757

Company Rule in India—1757

The Battle at Wandiwash—1760

Establishment of the Princely States—1765

The Regulating Act of 1773—1773

The Polygar Wars—1799

19th Century India

India's First Railway between Bombay and Thane is
Formed—1853

The First Three Universities of India is Established—
1857

Mahatma Gandhi is Born—1869

Queen Victoria Becomes Empress of India—1876

The National Congress of India is Founded—1885

20th Century in India

Delhi becomes the capital city of India—1911

India in World War I—1914-1918

Carnage at Amritsar—1919

India Gains Independence—1947

The Muslim League fights for a separate nation called Pakistan—1947

Mahatma Gandhi is Assassinated—1948

Indira Gandhi is Elected Prime Minister—1966

The First Nuclear Weapon of India is Detonated—1974

21st Century in India

India's Population exceeds 1 Billion—2000

Bill Clinton Visits India—2000

Tsunami kills over 10,000 People in India—2004

Mumbai Attack—2008

Introduction

India is a land in which the most ancient religions such as Hinduism, Buddhism and Jainism, originated. It is also a place in which the many cultures of the world— Greek, Persian and Central Asian— amalgamated to form hybrid cultures and religions such as the Greco-Buddhism and the Mahayana Buddhism.

This book relates 50 seminal events that helped sculpt modern India: the great empires that ruled, including the Mauryan Empire, Gupta Empire, Mughal Empire, Martha Empire; the Vedas; the Delhi Sultanate; the Battle of Plassey; the Taj Mahal and many more are discussed.

The eBook will enlighten you on India's most significant eras and events, from prehistoric to the present.

Prehistoric India

Archeological discoveries have proved that India was inhabited around 250,000 years ago during the Middle Pleistocene era. This makes the subcontinent one of the earliest regions of habitation.

India's prehistoric era is imbued with one of the earliest civilizations of the world, the Indus Valley Civilization. This era also saw the rise of great cities like the Mohenjo-Daro and Harappa, whose influence stretched to large territories of the subcontinent.

8000 B.C.

Stone Age India

In the central region of India, namely the Hathnora situated in the Narmada Valley, remnants of the Homo erectus were found. This is proof that the subcontinent was inhabited during the middle of the Iron Age—around 500,000 years ago. Relics of proto-humans dating as far back as 2.5 million years ago have also been uncovered.

It is believed that the fist semi-permanent settlements commenced in Bhimbetka - today's Madhya Pradesh - around 9,000 years ago.

The Mehrgarh discoveries (7000-9000 B.C.) and Bhirrana discoveries in Haryana (7500 B.C.) are proof of the Neolithic cultures that existed in South Asia.

5000 B.C.

Indus Valley Civilization Begins

India was named after the river Indus. Located near the Indus River and the adjacent areas (todays Pakistan and the north western regions of India), the Indus Valley civilization officially began around 3000 B.C. Archeological finds show that religious practices existed in the area around 5000 B.C. The earliest signs of agricultural settlements and urbanization were seen around the following century.

The Indus Valley Civilization is often dissected into three periods: Early (5000-4000 B.C.), Middle (4000-2900 B.C.) and Mature (2900-1900 B.C.).

Astonishingly, the inhabitants had a rather advanced life style. Excavation of the cities Harappa and Mohenjo-Daro prove that there were many homes with bathrooms, wells and even intricate systems of underground drainage.

Enforced with a well-structured system of urbanization, the social refinement of the region was superior to that of Egypt and Babylon (its contemporaries of civilization) and equivalent to that of the Sumerians.

It is also believed that the civilization had a writing of its own, often referred to as "Indus Script." Although the scripts have yet to be deciphered, texts were found on pottery, carved stamp seals, amulets and copper tablets recovered from the era.

There is also evidence that shows that this civilization had a close association with the Near East. Literary relics of Samaria, dated as far back as 2000 B.C., relate that the Indus River people (referred to as Meluhhaites by the Sumerian) had religious, commercial and artistic links with them. Here is an excerpt of a Sumerian document discussing the people of the Indus River:

The Meluhhaites, the men of the black land, bring to

Naram-Sin of Agae all kind of exotic wares"—

Haywood, The curse of Agade.

3000 B.C.

The Rise of Harappa

Located in today's Pakistan, namely the Punjab region, Harappa was the most celebrated city of the era. Harappa is another term for the Indus Valley Civilization; the city was established during the middle period of the civilization (3000 B.C.).

Harappa was, more or less, largely dismantled by the inhabitants in the later years, but it was critically damaged during the 19th century when much of the city's structure was taken and employed to build the foundations of the railroad being constructed by the British. Because of its early ruins, it is hard to assess the historical influence of the city. What is definite though is that Harappa carried an important Bronze Age community carrying a populace of 30,000.

The Harappans had their own religion and many deities; statues of the Shakti or the 'Mother Goddess' and Indra or the 'God of war and storm' are proof of their religious practices.

.

The Rise of Mohenjo-Daro

Mohenjo-Daro was located in the Sindh province (in today's Pakistan); it was established in 2600 B.C. during the mature periods of the civilization.

The city of Mohenjo-Daro (meaning 'Mount of the dead' in Sindhi), however, remained rather unscathed as a large part of it was buried until it was uncovered in the 20th century. As the finds of the Dancing Girl sculpted by independent seals show, the inhabitants had prowess over the use of bronze, copper and tin. The original name of the city is believed to be Kukkutarma (a Dravidian title meaning "the City of cock". This is perhaps because the city was a breeding ground for cocks or a location where cock-fighting was popular.

The cities of Harappa and Mohenjo-Daro became metropolises, spreading their civilization to over 250,000 settlements and cities throughout Pakistan, Afghanistan and large regions of Northern India. The large tracts of land in which the influence of these cities prevailed were larger than that of Mesopotamia and Egypt or its contemporaries put together.

Vedic India

According to some researchers, it was the Aryans that ushered in the Vedic Period (1500 B.C.-500 A.D.). At the center of the social order of this era was a pillar known as *The Vedas*, religious texts by which the society was structured. The people lead a pastoral lifestyle.

Despite the supreme influence of the Aryans, however, there were relics of the Indus Valley Civilization that endured during the Vedic Period and after. For instance, certain religious practices of parts of India and some of the Hindu deities trace as far back as the Indus Valley Civilization.

This era saw social stability and prosperity; social customs became incorporated into the day-to-day life of society. There also grew a centralized government.

The Rule of the Aryans

There was a wave of nomadic cattle-herders, known as the Aryans, who migrated from central Asia to India around 1500 B.C. Although it is often believed that it was the Aryans who brought the downfall of the Indus Valley Civilization, there are reasons to believe that the Civilization was decaying on its own for centuries.

The erosion is believed to have commenced around 1800 B.C. when the practice of writing began to vanish, the Near East networks became corrupted, certain cities were deserted and the use of standard gauging methods of weight and measurement for commercial and tax purposes became redundant. Reaching a decisive conclusion for why such an erosion of the civilization took place is quite difficult. Scholars postulate the drying of the Saraswati River as a factor; this commenced in 1900 B.C. Others, on the other hand, maintain that the region was struck by a devastating flood which destroyed the agriculture and led to an economic collapse. According to this argument, the expanse was unable to sustain independently and this eventually led to the split of the cities' civic structure. It is therefore argued that there was no invasion of the Aryans that led to the fall of the Indus Valley Civilization. As the civilization continued to erode, the Aryans gradually moved in, spreading their influence and going into the agricultural sector.

The Aryans are accredited for ushering in the Indo-European languages which are largely employed in today's South Asia. Modern India's social stratum and religious practices can be traced as far back as the Aryan migration and the indigenous people of Balathal.

1500-1100 B.C.

The Most Ancient Hindu Scriptures - The Vedas - are Penned

The Rig Veda, Atharva Veda, Yajur Veda, Sama Veda and other Hindu scriptures of antiquity were written during this era. The Vedas sculpted society; it was dissected into four social groups. This was commonly called 'the caste system' or the *Varnas*. These four castes included: the Brahmana, an elite group that comprised scholars and clerics; the Kshatriya, second to the elite class and a stratum of soldiers; the Shudra, a class of blue collars; and the Dalits, the underclass that were consigned to the disposal of waste and handling of meat—this is a class that was highly despised.

Initially the Varnas was a mere designation of one's occupation, but it evolved into a rigorous system in which one was cast into a social group from birth. Eventually, one was manacled to the caste he or she was born into; marriage between the different classes was also forbidden.

The religious values came to be known as Sanatan Dharma, meaning 'Eternal Order.' Having stemmed from the Indus River (Sindus River), this is a term that later came to be known as Hinduism, and its believers who thronged to the river for religious practices were called Sindus (and later Hindus).

The social order was redolent of the religious belief that was ordained by the supreme god Brahma (the Self). He was the deity responsible for the maintenance of the universe and for dictating the Eternal Order. The ideology of the Sanatan Dharma believed that the existence of the human life and the universe had a purpose;

therefore, by adhering to the Eternal Order, humanity lives a proper life.

The Upanishads—the Foundations of Hinduism—are Written

A set of philosophical and religious writings of Hinduism, the Upanishads are believed to have been authored between the 9th and 6th century BC. The scriptures are often called *Vedānta* (this either means "the object, the highest purpose of the Veda" or "last chapters, parts of the Veda").

During this epoch, the Indian society began to question the validity of the religious principles of the Vedas. A certain class of people even ventured in spiritual quests, leading a life of ascetic hermitage. They forsook family life and discarded the significance of material. And it is the discovery and philosophy of these spiritual pioneers that is scripted in the Upanishads. The collection seeks answers for many questions that are sought through spiritual quests.

The authors of the scriptures remain unknown. Sir Sarvepalli Radhakrishnan was the Indian philosopher and statesman (President of India from 1962 to 1967) who, through his master pieces such as the *Indian Philosophy* (1923-27), introduced the classical philosophy of India to the West. In discussing the authors of the Upanishads, he says, *"almost all the early literature of India was anonymous, we do not know the names of the authors of the Upanishads"*. Yajnavalkya, Aruni, Shandilya, Aitareya, Uddalaka and Shvetaketu are among the learned figures to whom the early philosophical theories of the Upanishads are attributed to.

500 B.C.

Buddhism is Founded 500 B.C.

During the 6th century B.C., India saw a rise of social and religious reforms. Progressives such as Siddhartha Gautama (563-483 B.C.) and Vardhaman Mahavira (599-527 B.C.) started to question the religious principles of The Vedas. They disaffiliated themselves from the conventional Sanatan Dharma and emerged with their own religions: Buddhism and Jainism. This was a significant part of the cultural and social uprisings the subcontinent saw during this epoch.

The Vedic religion, having been created nearly a millennium before the 6th century B.C., became outdated for the advanced society of the time. It was a religious system invented by a nomadic society and it was no fit for a non-nomadic society that supplanted the caravans of the nomadic people with agrarian settlements which in turn developed into villages, towns and then cities. The society grew more and more impatient with the backwards religious establishment; new religious ideologies challenging the Vedas became popular. It was amidst this social discontent that the godfather of Buddhism, Siddhartha Gautama, lived. He was born in Lumbini which is situated in today's Southern Nepal near the border of India and Nepal.

Discontent with the Vedic establishment, he founded a sect known as the Sangha; this was a group of lost ascetics referred to as the "Sramanas."

Following the death of Siddhartha Gautama, the Sramanas community developed into a religious movement around the 7th century B.C. With its roots centered in the renunciation of the world, the Vedic religion and the conventional establishment of society, the Sramanas movement became the progenitor of many religions and philosophical ideologies such as Buddhism and Jainism.

Jainism is Founded 500 B.C.

Often considered the sister of Buddhism, Jainism is a religious belief that rejects all worldly concerns and teaches the avenue to enlightenment and purity of the spirit. In Jainism, one must adhere to the disciplined lifestyle of ahimsa, a tradition that believes in a nonviolent approach towards all living creatures.

Vardhaman Mahavira is listed as last and 24th Tirthankara ("Ford Maker", a leader who shows the path from rebirth to salvation) and is known as Mahavira (meaning Great Hero). He is also posited as the final preacher of "right" faith, knowledge and practice. The first figure of the religion is believed to be Parshva or Parshvanatha.

The Persian Conquest (Achaemenid Rule)

The Persian Empire was reaching its pinnacle and sought to expand its territories. The increasing wealth and flourishing urbanization of India drew the attention of the Persian ruler, Cyrus the Great. So in 530 B.C., he ordered the invasion of the subcontinent. The conquerors entered through the northern regions of the Indus River and eventually permeated the southern region.

Persian rule (often referred to as the Achaemenid Empire) held large domains of India and its subjects lived under the customs and laws of the Persian Empire. Thinks were to remain this way until the 4th century B.C. when the rule of Persia was overthrown by another group of conquerors.

India Under Great Empires

From the 4ᵗʰ century B.C. to the 14ᵗʰ century A.D., the subcontinent saw the rise and fall of many great empires, including that of Alexander the Greats' empire, the Mauryan dynasty, the Kushan Empire, the Gupta Empire, the Dehli sultanate and many more.

A lot of foreign religions and cultures were introduced to the Indian population, and these had an enduring effect on the subcontinent. For instance, Persian rule structured new forms of governance, laying the administrative foundation for the Mauryan dynasty. Regions of northwest Pakistan and eastern Afghanistan became the site where Persian, Central Asian, Greek and Indian cultures amalgamated. This gave birth to hybrid-religions, cultures and kingdoms such as the Greco-Buddhism and Mahayana Buddhism and the Indo-Greek kingdom.

Alexander the Great Conquers India

Having conquered the Achaemenid Empire and Asia Minor, Alexander the Great moved on to the domains of the Persian Empire itself. In 326 B.C., he marched into Punjab with his Macedonian army and trounced King Porus in the Battle of Hydaspes. He moved further east but was repelled by Indian forces, namely the Gangaridai (Bengal) and the Nanda Empire (Magadha). Alexander's fatigued army had no appetite for another battle with Indian forces hailing from the Ganges River. The force rebelled at the Hyphasis and refused to advance further east.

After discussing the conundrum with Coenus, the chief officer, and after assessing the strength of the Nanda Empire, Alexander decided to withdraw his troop.

India was yet again infiltrated by foreign culture but continued to retain its earlier traits; this gave rise to the Greco-Buddhist culture. This culture stamped its imprint on the northern regions of the subcontinent's literature, clothing and arts. The reliefs and statues of the Buddha and others recovered from the era project a very Hellenic style of pose and dressing.

The Mauryan Empire is Established

In the wake of Alexander's departure, there followed the rise of another strong rule, the Mauryan Empire (322 B.C.- 185). It was founded by Chandragupta Maurya (322-298 B.C.); during the last periods of the 3rd century B.C., the kingdom held control of nearly all of the northern regions of India.

Maurya's successor and son, Bindusara (rule 298-272) pursued an expanding expedition of the dynasty's empire and secured domain throughout the whole of the subcontinent. He was succeeded by his son Ashoka the Great (304-232 B.C.); he was in power for nearly four decades, between 269-232 B.C.

Like his predecessors, Ashoka had the thirst of expanding the kingdoms territory. Eight years after his accession, he led a conquest to the city-state of Kalinga. The massive bloodletting of the conquest that claimed the lives of over 100,000 people traumatized Ashoka. He thus resorted to the practice of Buddhism.

For the rest of his tenure, Ashoka pursued a policy that advocated and prioritized the principles and teachings of Buddhism. He sponsored the building of many monasteries and funded Buddhist communities rather generously. These lavish expeditions were not without implications: the nation's coffer was exhausted and, following Ashoka's death, the empire saw a rapid collapse.

30 B.C.

The Kushan Empire is Established

Following the demise of the Mauryan Empire, there followed a rise of small empires and kingdoms. The Kushan Empire (30 B.C.-240 A.D.) was among those powers.

The kingdom had extensive commercial networks that included Rome and China. The era saw a lot of prosperity and growth in urban life, art and Buddhist practices.

In discussing the establishment of the Kushan Empire (Guishuang as the Chinese call them), Ban Yong, a Chinese general, writes to his Emperor as follows:

"More than a hundred years later (than the conquest of Bactria by the Da Yuezhi), the prince (xihou) of Guishuang (Badakshan) established himself as king, and his dynasty was called that of the Guishuang (Kushan) King. He invaded Anxi (Indo-Parthia), and took the Gaofu (Kabul) region. He also defeated the whole of the kingdoms of Puda (Paktiya) and Jibin (Kapisha and Gandhara). Qiujiuque (Kujula Kadphises) was more than eighty years old when he died. His son, Yangaozhen [probably Vema Tahk(tu) or, possibly, his brother Sadaṣkaṇa], became king in his place. He defeated Tianzhu [North-western India] and installed Generals to supervise and lead it. The Yuezhi then became extremely rich. All the kingdoms call [their king] the Guishuang [Kushan] king, but the Han call them by their original name, Da Yuezhi."

-Hou Hanshu.

The Gupta Empire Begins (The Golden Age of India)

Sri Gupta ('Sri' meaning 'Lord') is believed to have established the Gupta Empire (320-550 A.D.). He reigned for four decades between the years 240 and 280. Sri Gupta is an emblem that defied the caste system, which dictated the every facet of the subcontinent's citizens. He rose to power despite the barriers of his class (a merchant or Vaishya). He established a system of governance that fostered stability and growth of literature, science, astronomy, philosophy, engineering, mathematics and much besides.

The *Puranas of Vysa*, the celebrated caves of Ellora and Ajanta were products of this era.

In these caves, there is a dominance of Buddhist art works than those of Hindu; this was because the originator of the kingdom and his successors were advocates of Buddhism and they propagated its establishment as a national religion.

India is Conquered by Muslims

The Gupta Empire continued to erode until its final collapse in the 6th century; it was followed by the reign of Harsha Vardhan (590-647 A.D.). A devout Buddhist yet an indisputable warrior, Harsha Vardhan was a great leader that brought the prosperity of Northern India.

That prosperity ceased to exist after his death. India descended into complete chaos and split into smaller kingdoms. The unity needed to fend off foreign invasion was absent, and so the subcontinent was exposed to the imminent invasion: the Muslim invasion of 712 A.D., spearheaded by Muhammed bin Quasim. This conquest annexed Northern India (today's Pakistan) in to the Muslim Empire.

Muslim control demolished the native rule of India and a system in which communities and self-governing city states fell under the authority of one city was introduced.

The Delhi Sultanate

From the 13th to 16th century, the Delhi sultanate emerged as the Muslim sovereign of North India. With its fortress in Delhi, the kingdom spread its domains throughout India. The kingdom ruled for over three centuries and five successive dynasties ruled: (1206-1290 A.D.) the Mamluk Dynasty, (1290-1320) the Khilji Dynasty, (1320-1414) the Tughlaq Dynasty—these were the four dynasties that were of Turkic origin. The last sultanate dynasty was the Afghan Lodi Dynasty that reigned from 1451-1526.

16th Century India

The 16th century was a rather eventful era in India for it was a period that bore witness to the first successful European invasion and settlement; it was the era in which India saw the rise and fall of her great empire. The 16th century in India was simply a time of gory battles and bloodshed.

1503

The First European Settlement in India

The first siege of the city Cochin (otherwise known as Kochi) is said to be an event that marked the first European settlement in India. And it all began when the Zamorin Raja of Calicut began to seek out Portuguese agents in Cochin. The agents were under the protection of Cochin's Trimumpara Raja. When Zamorin knew about this arrangement, he demanded for Trimumpara Raja to deliver these agents to him as prisoners.

Trimumpara Raja had established a good relationship with the Portuguese. And so the emperor stoutly refused to submit. This response triggered a war between the two empires.

Zamorin then joined forces with the Malabari and the siege of Cochin commenced. Zamorin's army was greater than that of Trimumpara's, so Cochin's downfall seemed inevitable. But then the Portuguese, with the command of Francisco de Albuquerque, arrived at Cochin with the 5th Armada.

At this juncture Zamorin's army along with the allies, the Malabari, decided that it was time to restructure, and so they immediately resorted to a temporary retreat.

During this hiatus, the Portuguese began to immediately strengthen Cochin's defense system. And they eventually asked to establish a fort of their own on Cochin's coastline (Fort Kochi, as it is now known).

Trimumpara Raja was basically at the whims of the Portuguese, and so it didn't take much time for him to allow the formation of this fortress. He even went as far as providing them will all the needed material.

The fortress was completed in a matter of months and it's known to be one that marked the first European settlement in India.

Battle of Diu

The 16th century in India is generally known to be a period of chaos, war and colonization. And nothing could possibly highlight these elements more than the Battle of Diu.

The Battle of Diu (otherwise known as the Second Battle of Chaul), took place in 1509 on February 3rd, not far from the coast of Diu. It was a naval warfare between the Portuguese Empire and the Mamluk Sultanate of Egypt, the Sultanate of Gujarat and the Zamorin Raja of Calicut. The latter were supported by the Republic of Venice, the Ottoman Empire and the Republic of Ragusa.

The battle was initially purposed for Portugal to further expand and fortify her dominating presence in Asia. But then it became personal when Francisco de Almeida, commander of the Portuguese fleet, learned of his son's killing by the Mirocem.

The Portuguese entered the sea battle with about 1,500 soldiers and eighteen well accoutered vessels. They were also assisted by the Emperor of Cochin, who sent about four hundred men. The joined fleet of the Sultanates and Zamorin were certainly massive, but their soldiers weren't well trained and their artillery was far weaker than that of the Portuguese.

The battle was long and certainly gory and it ended on November 1509 with the Portuguese coming out as the victor.

1510

Establishment of Portuguese India

Claiming victory at the Battle of Diu made Portugal a force to be reckoned with in India; for it was an event that paved the way for the establishment of Portuguese India in 1510.

After the triumph at the Battle of Diu, the Portuguese empire selected Afonso de Albuquerque as the empire's second governor in East India. The new governor then deployed a reinforced fleet to Calicut and ordered them to demolish the Zamorin Empire. The army, commanded by Fernão Coutinho, did manage to siege the palace and tear it down; they also set the entire city ablaze. But the Emperor escaped.

Then in the year 1510, with the assistance of the Hindu Vijayanagara Empire and the Timayya, Governor Afonso de Albuquerque and his army was able to defeat the Bijapur Sultans. And this victory allowed the Portuguese to settle permanently in Old Goa, otherwise known as Velha Goa, Southern Province, Goa or as the Europeans called it 'Rome of the East.'

Goa then became the headquarters of Portuguese State of India, and the expansion of territory began from then on. Portuguese India subsisted until 1961.

1526

Rise of the Mughal Empire

The Mughal Empire came into being in 1526, when Babur, the founder of the empire, defeated Ibrahim Lodi in the Battle of Panipat and became ruler of Northern India.

Babur was a descendant of the Timurid Dynasty, with blood relations to both the founder of the Timurid Empire, Timur, and the founder of the Mongol Empire, Genghis Khan.

The Mughal Empire enjoyed a vast expanse of territory in both India and Middle East; the Bengal region, Afghanistan and the Gangetic Plain were but a few.

But when Babur was succeeded by his son, Humayun, in 1530, the Empire reached the brink of its downfall. Not long after this new empire began to set its root in India, Sher Khan Sur assembled a group of rebels and forced Humayun to flee India and seek refuge in Persia.

But then in 1555, Humayun amassed his army, defeated Sher Khan Sur and claimed back his rightful throne. However, Humayun didn't live long enough to enjoy his victory or empire, because he was killed in an accident in 1556.

Akbar the Great, Emperor of the Mughal Empire

Akbar acceded to the throne in 1556, when his father, Humayun died a sudden death. History describes Akbar, which means 'Great,' as one of the greatest rulers of the Mughal Empire.

His skills in managing matters dealing with war and diplomacy, led the Kingdom to its Classical Era. Northern India under the ruling of Akbar the Great enjoyed a great expanse of territory, economic development, social enhancement and much besides. Art, literature and architecture in India saw a rise hitherto unknown. With Akbar as the head, the Mughal Empire became a Kingdom to be reckoned with.

Akbar was also a stout advocate of religious freedom; he permitted the "free expression of religion" and tried spreading the custom of religious and cultural tolerance in society.

The emperors of the Mughal Empire were all Muslims. And Akbar became the first in the Kingdom to convert and become a devout follower of a religion he himself brought into formation "Din-i-Ilahi."

Akbar died in 1605 and was succeeded by his son Jahangir. The Mughal Empire lasted until 1707.

17th Century India

The 17th century was a time that saw a conglomerate of events. It was the period in which European East India Companies were established; the magnificent Taj Mahal was completed and the Martha Empire came into being.

Formation of the East India Company

"It originated from sub-scriptions, trifling in amount, of a few private individuals. It gradually became a commercial body with gigantic resources, and by the force of unforeseen circumstances assumed the form of a sovereign power,"

– Bentley

The East India Company, which was also called The John Company or the Honorable East India Company, came into formation in 1600 on December 31st.

When the Portuguese and Spanish monopoly dissolved in 1588 and the Indian Ocean, the Atlantic and the Pacific Ocean were open for merchants to trade, a group of affluent British business men assembled and decided to establish a joint-stock company.

Trade with the East Indies was known to be the most lucrative business of the century. So the group invested all they had in this pursuit and presented the proposal to Queen Elizabeth for final approval. And after much convincing and persistence, the Queen granted the visionary merchants the Royal Charter.

The Royal Charter, which was then titled "Governor and Company of Merchants of London trading with the East Indies," was granted to Earl of Cumberland, George, Burgesses, Aldermen and 215 knights.

The company is known to establish its first factory Bantam on its first trip to India.

British India

The whole of India officially became a British Colony in the mid-19th century. But British dominance in India began in the 17th century when the East India Company established itself on Indian soil.

At the time the EIC arrived in India, the Mughal Empire still had a stronghold. Then the British merchants found a way to get the Emperor's approval to build a trading station at a port located on the north-west coast, Surat.

The formation of this new trading station raged the Portuguese and that lead to several hostile confrontations and sea battles. Then in 1612 the British Merchants and the Portuguese engaged at the Battle of Swally. The British came out victorious and asserted their superiority in India.

Then as the Mughal Empire grew more decadent and fragile, the British East India Company began to seize more power and strength in India. It didn't take long before the company began to expand its trading operations and open factories in the cities that promised success.

Then the company began to seek out military power and started to recruit soldiers. In 1778, the British East India Company had an army of about 67,000 soldiers. There were certainly several rulers that opposed the presence of this company and its pervasive nature, but no one was strong enough to confront it and India eventually fell under the rule of the East India Company.

Then in 1873 the British Empire stepped in and dissolved the company, claiming rights to its army and the nation itself.

1642

French India

The French got their hands on the renowned East India trade decades after the Dutch and English. The French East India Company or La Compagnie française des Indes orientales was established in 1642.

Much like the way other European powers seized their colonial territories in India, the French were also able to colonize parts of India because of the French East India Company.

The corporation's first expedition to India was in 1668. The sail was marshaled by François Caron. Their destination was Surat and on that same year the French erected their first factory on Indian soil.

Then on the following year the French managed to establish another factory in Masulipatam. Step by step the French were able to secure their presence in India, creating an alliance with the ruler of India and building factories and forts in major cities such as Chandannagar, Bantam, Pondichéry and so forth.

But the Dutch and English, which were the greatest European forces in India, made it very difficult for the French to sustain their position. Then in 1769, due to lack of finance, the French Crown decided to dissolve the French East India Company and assume all of its possessions.

Completion of the Taj Mahal

"O Soul, thou art at rest. Return to the Lord at peace with Him, and

He at peace with you"

— reads the Great Gate.

The Taj Mahal, which is also known as "the Crown of Palaces" is one of India's most prized possessions, an entity that says quite a lot about India's history.

The heads of the Mughal Empire are known to be stout advocates of art and architecture, and the Taj Mahal stands as a testament. This magnificent edifice was authorized and funded by the fifth emperor of the Mughal Empire, Shah Jahan, in 1628.

The Taj Mahal was initially built as a burial chamber for the Emperor's wife, Mumtaz Mahal. Over 20,000 professionals, including several architects who were managed by Ustad Ahmad Lahauri, labored on this project. The project was completed in

1653 with an estimated expenditure of about 32 million Indian rupees.

The Taj Mahal is located in the city Agra. It is about 240 feet high and is made out of white marble and semi-precious gemstones.

The Taj Mahal is certainly a relic that continues to marvel the world. It attracts about 3 million tourists on a yearly basis, it's listed as one of UNESCO's World Heritage Site and it has claimed one of the trophies in the 2007 New Seven Wonders of the World award.

1674

Establishment of the Maratha Empire

The Maratha Empire, otherwise known as the Mahratta Confederacy, was founded by Chatrapati Shivaji Raje Bhosale in 1674. The empire was composed of Hindus hailing from Maharashtra (otherwise known as Western Deccan Plateau).

The Empire came into being when Shivaji along with his supporters rose to resist the Mughal Empire. Soon after Shivaji and his army grew strong, they formed a Hindavi Swarajya, which means "self-rule of the Hindu People." The insurgents then seized the city Raigad from the Mughal Empire and made it their capital city. From then on the Martha Empire became a sovereign Kingdom in India.

It wasn't long before this newly formed empire became a force to be reckoned with. It defended its Kingdom from enemy forces; expanded its territories to as far as Bengal in the East, Peshawar in the North to Tamil Nadu in the south; claimed victory in several battles with the Mughals, the Portuguese, the English, the Dutch and much more.

The Martha Empire is also known to be the cause that brought about the downfall of the Mughal Empire. The kingdom endured until it became a British colony in 1818.

After a devastating loss at the Third Battle of Panipat, the empire became a confederacy. Weakened by this division the Martha Empire was then repeatedly defeated by the British army at the Anglo-Maratha wars, which eventually lead to its ruins.

Danish India

Danish India is a title used in reference to the territories that both Norway and Denmark colonized. The duo arrived in India in 1620 with Admiral Ove Gjuedde as commander.

Much like other European merchants, the Danish-Norwegian pursuit in India was solely purposed on getting a share of the lucrative trading business. But they didn't have the finance or military power to succeed as that of the British, Portuguese or the Dutch East India Companies.

But the fact that they had a fragile presence in India helped them evade various confrontations. And that paved the way to the sustenance of their colonies in India for about two centuries.

Their colonies included West Bengal, Tamil Nadu and Nicobar Islands. Danish India and the Danish East India Company came to an end in 1845, when the British progressively took control of all their colonies.

18th Century India

The 18th century was a time of war and bloodshed in India. It was the period in which the British assumed complete control over this nation. And in response to this dominance an ample of resistance rose, which resulted in thousands of casualties.

1757

Battle of Plassey

The Battle of Plassy took place in 1757 on June 23rd. It was a rather minor conflict that lasted for just a couple of hours. Its sudden conclusion though didn't make it less important for the British, for it was the very event that helped assert their rights and strength on Indian soil.

The confrontation occurred at the former capital city of Bengal, Plassey (otherwise known as Palashi). The conflict was between the British East India Company and the Nawab of Bengal, Siraj-ud-Daulah, who had the support of the French East India Company and Bihar and Orissa.

When the British East India Company began to secure its place in areas surrounding the city of Bengal, the Nawab Siraj-ud-Daulah grew suspicious and decided to launch an attack on Calcutta (an area under British control). In response to this attack the British Admiral Charles Watson, dispatched an army to recapture Calcutta. The troops were marshaled by Colonel Robert Clive.

Hearing of this conflict, the French, wanting to oust the British from India, sent out a small force to the Nawab of Bengal. Unnerved by this alliance the British Colonel Robert Clive then managed to bribe the commander of Siraj-ud-Daulah's army, Mir Jafar, promising to make him the Nawab of Bengal if he complied.

This conspiracy gave the British more leverage and eventually helped them claim victory at the Battle of Plassey.

1757

Company Rule in India

The British East India Company is known to arrive in India in the early 17th century. But it became a force strong enough to recruit its own soldiers, collect tax from locals and literally became the ruler of the whole nation after their triumph at the Battle of Plassey in 1757.

After the devastating defeat at the Battle of Plassey, Siraj-ub-daulah, the Nawab of Bengal, was left with no other choice but to surrender his territories. As a result of this battle, the British were also able to seize Chandernagar (a fort of the French).

With the annexation of Bengal and Carnatic the company then grew affluent, and with that extra finance the British rushed to recruit more soldiers. They eventually became a military might; far greater and stronger than any other European power in India.

And by instituting puppet governments everywhere, the EIC progressively managed to gain complete authority over each town in India.

This was the era in which India had a company as a ruler, and this dominance lasted until 1858.

The Battle at Wandiwash

The Battle at Wandaiwash took place in 1760 on January 22nd, at the time of the Seven Year' War. The conflict was between the French and the British, and the two forces engaged at the city, Vandavasi (now known as Tamil Nadu).

The Battle at Wandaiwash had very little significance for the British, as they already gained all the power they wanted by annexing Bengal after the Battle of Plassy. But for the French, this battle was very deceive, as it was an event that decided upon the fate of the French East India Company.

The British, knowing they had the finance and accouterment to face the French in battle, decided to attack them in Vandavasi (also called Wandaiwash). The French on the other hand were not only underfunded but they also had to deal with little or no military support from the French Crown.

The French army, which was commanded by Count de Lally, fought of the British for as long and as much as was possible. But the French were eventually defeated and their territories were seized. They surrendered in 1761 on January 16th and the British army was under the command of Sir Eyre Coote.

Establishment of the Princely States

In 1765 India officially became a British colony. But even after the British hailed over this massive nation and proclaimed to be the sole rulers of India, there were still towns and provinces that sustained their sovereignty. And these territories came to be known as Princely States, or Indian State.

The Princely States were said to be about 565; Hyderabad, Jammuand Kashmir, Mysore and Baroda, were the strongest of them all.

As agreed upon in a treaty between the British government and the Princely states, the British possessed complete authority over the external affairs of these sovereign states, in regards to internal affairs, however, the Princely states were allowed to do as they please. But of course, for this practice the British imposed certain restrictions:

"The treaties with most of the larger States are clear on this point. Posts in the interior must not be fortified, factories for the production of guns and ammunition must not be constructed, nor may the subject of other States be enlisted in the local forces. ... They must allow the forces that defend them to obtain local supplies, to occupy cantonments or positions, and to arrest deserters; and in addition to these services they must recognize the Imperial control of the railways, telegraphs, and postal communications as essential not only to the common welfare but to the common defense"

— The treaty

The Regulating Act of 1773

The Regulating Act of 1773 was issued by the Parliament of Great Britain so as to effectively manage the East India Company.

The British East India Company was one of Britain's greatest revenue streamlines. To sustain the trading monopoly, the company paid its government a yearly amount of £400,000. But at the time this legislation was instituted, this corporation was going through a great amount of trouble financially, and was unable to pay its fines due.

The company was then soaked in debt; it owed money - over £1.5 million - to both the government and the Bank of England. And this act allowed the government to have a better insight and hand on the company's work.

Shareholders opposed the Act, as it limited the Court of Directors to only four years and minimized the company's dividends to 6%. The act didn't subsist for long, but it did pave the way for the British Crown to dissolve it in 1873.

The Polygar Wars

The Polygar Wars, which is also known as the Palayaikarar Wars, was a conflict that took place twice between the British forces and the Polygars (otherwise known as Palaiyakkarars), who hailed from the earlier empire of Tamil Nadu, the Tirunelvele Kingdom.

The first conflict took place in 1799, when in a meeting over taxation, the British and the Nayak of Panchalakurichi, Kattabomman, got into a disagreement and opened fire. The commander of the British army got killed in this event.

In response to this killing the British sent out their troops to Panchalakurichi to capture Kattabomman. After a lot of struggle the British managed to defeat Kattabomman and his army. The leader, along with his close ally, Subramania Pillai, was then trialed and hanged in the public square, for this was meant to terrorize the mass.

The British then went on to further terrorize the locals, but this ended up causing more rebellion than had been expected. Then in

1800, a group of rebels attacked the British fort in Coimbatore and the Second Polygar War broke out.

The Second Polygar War took more than a year to come to a conclusion, as the Polygars were then joined by a lot of forces. The British won the battle at the end, but only after a long and arduous struggle and a mind numbing expenditure.

19th Century India

The 19th century was a fundamental year for India. The first railway and three universities were established, the Indian National Congress was founded and one of the most revered and influential figure of our world, Mahatma Gandhi, was born.

India's First Railway between Bombay and Thane is Formed

It was in the mid-19th century that India's history of rail transport commenced. There existed no railway lines in India before 1850; but it all changed three years later.

The first commercial railway from Bombay to Thane was established on the 16th of April, 1853. Gradually, railways were developed by the British East India Company (for some time) and later by the British Colonial Government. It was at first to convey armies for their many wars and second for the transportation of cotton for export.

Robert Maitland Brereton, an engineer from Britain, was responsible for expanding the railways after 1857.In 1864, the "Calcutta-Allahabad-Delhi" line was finished and the East Indian Railway Allahabad-Jabalpur branch line opened in 1867.

The investment on the railways in India by British corporations reached around £95 million by 1875. Later, it transpired that the corruption level in these investments were rather high from both the companies who supplied steel and machinery in Britain and the members of the Colonial British Government in India. This eventuated in the increase of the price of railway equipment and lines.

1857

The First Three Universities of India is Established

The first three universities in India to have been built were the University of Mumbai, Madras and Calcutta in 1857. They were established by the British there.

The formation was initiated in 1835 when the "President of the General Committee of Public Instruction" and "Law Member in Government," Macaulay, wrote about how he strongly favored English education in India. So, it was decided by the Court of Directors to build universities at Calcutta and Bombay resembling that of London University. They also agreed to open one more at Madras or somewhere else in India.

1869

Mahatma Gandhi is Born

On October 2nd, 1869, Mohandas Karamchand Gandhi was born in Porbandar, India. The chief minister of Porbandar was Gandhi's father, Karamchand Gandhi (*alias* Kaba Gandhi). Putlibai was his mother. *"She was deeply religious"* Gandhi states in his autobiography when mentioning his mother. He also adds that eating *"without her daily prayers"* was out of the question.

Gandhi grew up following the ancient Indian religion Jainism that was pro-fasting, vegetarianism meditation, but most of all non-violence.

Gandhi was introvert as a young boy and was a mediocre student. He was also very timid as a teenager and he never slept without turning the lights on. He was married to Kasturba Makanji, both at the age of thirteen, in an arranged marriage.

He took up on the opportunity to study law overseas in England in 1888, at the age of 18. Transitioning to Western culture was a struggle for him at first, but during his years in London, his commitment to a diet devoid of meat and abstinence from sex and alcohol solidified. During his stay, he also began to read scriptures of other religions including Buddhism, Christianity, Hinduism and others, to further his knowledge about them.

When he came back to India in 1891, he heard of the devastating news that his mother passed away just weeks before his arrival.

As a lawyer, his trepidation was a deterrent factor. His first courtroom case ended badly when Gandhi, overwhelmed with anxiety, couldn't think of any questions to ask when it was time to cross-examine a witness. He made haste to leave the Court and reimbursed the legal fee to his client. Gandhi decided not to tackle anymore projects until he summoned his courage and he didn't accomplish that until he went to South Africa.

Gandhi sailed for South Africa in 1893, to conduct legal services. When he arrived there though, he was promptly repulsed by the discrimination immigrants from India faced by the Boer and British authorities. He also encountered racial segregation firsthand on different occasions, which furthered his battle against discrimination and his desire for justice. In 1894, he established the National Indian Congress to do just that.

1876

Queen Victoria Becomes Empress of India

The conservative Prime Minister, Benjamin Disraeli, assumed power again after the general election in 1874. Disraeli put forward The Royal Titles Act 1876 to Parliament to entitle Queen Victoria the "Empress of India." There was a ceremony held at Delhi

Durbar after the announcement of the new title on January 1st, 1877.

The National Congress of India is Founded

The Indian National Congress is one of the oldest political parties in the world and it was founded in 1885. It was the Theosophical Society's members which founded the congress. Alan Octavian Hume was the first to arrange the Congress meeting in 1885. The session saw the attendance of 72 delegates including: W.C. Bannerjee, Justice Ranade, Dadabhai Naoroji, Pherozeshah Mehta, Dinshaw Wacha and K.T. Telang. There was, however, a prevalent belief among the Indian society that the political party was formed to shift the lasting disgruntlement among the population of India over the British rule into something more positive.

The Indian National Congress in its twenty years after being formed saw the domination of leaders known as the "Moderates." These moderates were pro progress which was orderly. But there was an emergence of an opponent group by 1907, which were known as the "Extremists"; this group's approach towards the rule of Britain was aggressive.

One of the most prominent amongst the "Extremists" was Bal Gangadhar Tilak. In 1907, when he was addressing the Congress, demanding to boycott the goods from Britain and to fight the British control stated that:

"Two new words have recently come into existence with regard to our politics, and they are Moderates and Extremists. These words have a specific relation to time, and they, therefore, will change with time. The Extremists of today will be Moderates tomorrow, just as the Moderates of today were Extremists yesterday. When the National Congress was first started and Mr. Dadabhai's views, which now go for Moderates, were given to the public, he was styled an Extremist, so that you will see that the term Extremist is an expression of progress."

20th Century in India

The 20th century was indeed a milestone for India— its independence from the British Empire and the first female Prime Minister, Indira Gandhi, of India being the highlights of the period. But India also lost one of its illustrious figures during that century, Mahatma Gandhi.

1911

Delhi becomes the Capital City of India

On December 12, 1911, the capital city of India became New Delhi. Calcutta was the capital before 1911. The main ground to changing the capital city from Calcutta to Delhi was its location. Calcutta was located in the east coast of India, while Delhi was situated in the north area. The British administration in the county believed that it was more convenient to rule India from Delhi.

The news of the capital changing to Kolkata to Delhi was declared on December 12, 1911, by the then ruling Emperor of India, George V.

Edwin Lutyens and Herbert Baker, two of the most leading British architects then, were selected for the first arrangement and structural design for Delhi. Construction work commenced once the plan was authorized and the city was finally inaugurated by Lord Irwin, Viceroy of India then, on February 13, 1931. There were also plans proposed to enlarge the city and various architects shared their ideas though most of them were declined due to the massive expense.

India in World War I

India's contribution in terms of army supplies was massive in World War I. The troops that were sent out from India were over a million. Soldiers to the tune of 74,187 died during the war, whereas 67,000 troops sustained injury.

It was against the German Empire in German East Africa that the Indian Army was fighting. The divisions of India were also dispatched to Gallipoli, Egypt and Mesopotamia. The remaining soldiers had to guard the North West Frontier of India.

Sir Claude Auchinleck, Field-Marshal and the Indian Army's chief officer from 1942, declared that the British *"couldn't have come through both wars [WWI and WWII] if they hadn't had the Indian Army."*

Carnage at Amritsar

On April 13, several Indians marched on the streets of Amritsar to meet at a city park called Jallianwala Bagh to protest the heavy war levy imposed on the people of India by the British administration and the involuntary enlistment of the Indian soldiers. The troops of Britain and India gunned down as many as 379 demonstrators, many of which were Indian nationalists.

Just a few days prior to the massacre, there was a large protest held at Amritsar and Brigadier-General Reginald Dyer announced that all rally in the city was prohibited and also threatened to disperse a crowd even if it means by force.

Jallianwala Bagh, however, was attended by thousands of demonstrators; many of them were uninformed of the new ban on public gatherings. They were caught by surprise when the troops of Dyer, who encircled the park, started firing at the mob without any warning. This event cost the lives of hundreds of protestors and thousands to be injured.

Dyer ordered the withdrawal of his army, leaving the dead and injured on the ground.

The atrocious news stirred massive condemnation. Winston Churchill rebuked *"an extraordinary event, a monstrous event, an event which stands in singular and sinister isolation."*

The censured Dyer was later forced by the British to resign from his post.

This event had deeply affected Mahatma Gandhi, who, during the First World War, showed vigorous support for the British hoping for India to gain partial independence. Following the carnage however, Gandhi's stance on seeking full independence for his mother land didn't waver. To accomplish that, he began his first crusade against the oppressive British rule in India— the Civil Disobedience Movement.

India Gains Independence

After struggling a great deal socially and politically, India finally gained Independence on 15 August, 1947. The British controlled India for a long period of time. Though their initial objection was only trade related, after a while, the desire for administrative and political control began to develop.

Much of India's internal affairs were controlled by the British India Company. Several Indians harbored resentment towards British rule; they desired a land of their own where the distribution of equal rights prevailed. National leaders such as Mahatma Gandhi, Vallabhai Patel, Pandit Jawaharlal Nehru and many others stoutly and relentlessly struggled for the governmental and political rights of Indians. The British dealt with those who fought for the rights of Indians in a rather callous fashion, frequently playing the "divide and rule" game. This created a gap between the Muslims and the Hindus thus forming the Muslim League.

The force of the National Movement in India was getting stronger in the 1920s. There were many movements started by Mahatma Gandhi in opposition to the British including the Non-cooperation Movement (1920-1922) and the Civil Disobedience Movement. The campaigns for independence persisted through the 1930s; however, it was during WWII that it gained grounds. The Indian National Congress partnered with the British during war, hoping that they would finally get out of India following the Second World War. This proved wrong though, as the British had a strong stance. This led to Gandhi creating the "Quit India Movement" in 1942. Eventually, the great deeds of Nationalists like Mahatma Gandhi served as a reminder for the British to make alterations and ultimately allow India independence. In 1947, India became an independent state.

The Muslim League fights for a separate nation called Pakistan

Following the withdrawal of the British from India in 1947, the Muslim League's main concern was that the Hindus would gain most of the leadership position in internal affairs. This sentiment amongst the League persisted despite the proposed plan to divide power between Hindus and Muslims, thus they sought for a separate land, Pakistan.

Gandhi was against partition and proposed that Mohammad Ali Jinnah, the chief of the Muslim League, should lead the united India. Several important figures, however, didn't hesitate to express their objection to this idea. The British Parliament, finally, ratified the Indian Independence Act which eventuated in the establishment of India and Pakistan.

Mahatma Gandhi is Assassinated

Prior to independence, Muslims and Hindus often clashed; though the bloodshed exacerbated after August 15, 1947. Gandhi frequented areas devastated by the riots in seek of peace. To put an end to the slaughter the Mahatma (meaning "great soul") fasted. Gandhi's compassion towards the Muslims was misinterpreted by some Hindus as an act of a traitor.

During a prayer meeting on January 30, 1948, Nathuram Godse, a Hindu extremist, shot the 78-year-old Mahatma Gandhi three times with a pistol. Mahatma was still feeble from recurring hunger strikes. Though Gandhi constantly preached and supported non-violence, his life was taken by a vicious act.

In November 1949, Gandhi's assassin and co-conspirator were put to death by hanging.

Gandhi, even after his death, inspired several people throughout the world to adhere to non-violence when struggling for freedom including the civil rights leaders Martin Luther King Jr. and Nelson Mandela.

Indira Gandhi is Elected Prime Minister

Indira Gandhi, on January 19, 1966, became the first female Prime Minister of India. Also Jawaharlal Nehru's only daughter, Indira Gandhi gained extensive support from the public for the great improvements she made in agriculture which resulted in India's independent production of food grain. Her success in the war between Pakistan, which led to the formation of Bangladesh in 1971, also garnered her massive support.

Indira Gandhi was, nevertheless, voted out of office following the three terms she served for her increasingly severe rules; but she was re-elected to serve for the fourth time.

On the 31st of October, 1984, two bodyguards of Indira Gandhi assassinated her.

The First Nuclear Weapon of India is Detonated

Indira Gandhi, on September 7, 1972, gave authorization to the Bhabha Atomic Research Center (BARC) to produce a nuke for a test. India called this device the *"Peaceful Nuclear Explosive"* though often denoted as the *"Smiling Buddha."*

India detonated its first nuclear device (the Smiling Buddha test) On May 18, 1974. Every facet of the preparation was tightly controlled by Indira Gandhi. The test was carried out in great confidentiality and in addition to Gandhi, only counselors Durga Dhar and Parmeshwar Haksar were informed about it.

According to Scholar Raj Chengappa, Jagjivan Ram, the Indian Defense Minister, didn't know about the nuclear test until it was already detonated. The Minister of External Affairs, Swaran Singh, was given notice just 2-days in advance. The civilian scientists who were employed by the Indian government didn't exceed seventy-five.

Pakistan's perspective over the "peaceful nuclear explosion" was quite the opposite. In June 1974, the Prime Minister of Pakistan, Zulfikar Ali Bhutto, pleaded to never submit to "nuclear blackmail" or succumb to "Indian hegemony or domination over the subcontinent." Munir Ahmed Khan, chairman of Pakistan Atomic Energy Commission, stated that the test would only drive Pakistan to experiment with its own nuclear weapon.

21st Century in India

Though we have yet to see what the rest of the 21st century holds for India, it has so far seen success as well as struggles.

India's Population exceeds 1 Billion

On March 1, 2000, it was announced that the population of India was estimated to be around 1.2 billion, making it the second nation after China to pass "the billion mark." In 1991, India's populace was 846 million.

After India became an independent state, the average life expectancy grew from 39-years to 63-years.

Although the administration has tried to encourage the population of India to limit its family size, it didn't take austere measures like China by restricting its people to a one-child-per-family policy.

Bill Clinton Visits India

In 2000, Bill Clinton made a trip to India. He was the first president to visit India since Jimmy Carter's tour in 1978. The trip marked Washington's new objective to make the political and economical ties stronger with India.

Atal Behari Vajpayee, the Prime Minister of India, and the US President signed a "Joint vision statement" for the 21st century which promised to generate *"closer and qualitatively new relationship between India and the United States."*

A topic that was also covered widely was nuclear weapons:

"India and the United States share a commitment to reducing and ultimately eliminating nuclear weapons, but we have not always agreed on how to reach this common goal. The United States believes India should forgo nuclear weapons. India believes that it needs to maintain a credible minimum nuclear deterrent in keeping with its own assessment opposition of its security needs. Nonetheless, India and the US are prepared to work together to prevent the

proliferation of nuclear weapons and their means of delivery. To this end, we will persist with and build upon the productive bilateral dialogue already underway."

2004

Tsunami kills over 10,000 People in India

On December 26ᵗʰ, 2004, an Indian Ocean earthquake, recorded as "one of the ten worst earthquakes in history," triggered a tsunami wave that was responsible for the death of many people in parts of Indonesia, India, South and Southeast Asia, Thailand and Sri Lanka, making the overall casualties 230,000.

There were various names given to the tsunami including the "South Asian tsunami", "2004 Indian Ocean tsunami", "Indonesian tsunami", "Boxing Day tsunami" and the "Christmas tsunami."

The tsunami hit the different states of India including two of the most devastated states Tamil Nadu and Kerala; Andhra Pradesh was also hit by the tsunami, though it was to a moderate level.

Other states included Kakinada, Visakhapatnam, Tuticorin, Chennai, Marmagoa and Kochi.

The confirmed death toll in India reached 12,405.

The 2004 tsunami left nothing but distress on the population and government of India. And to exacerbate the situation, the Indian administration, four days after the Asian Tsunami, was warned by a US-based company, that the coastal areas of India might be struck again by a tsunami in the next twelve hours. The Indian minister of Home Affairs quickly informed the public, which engendered panic in the regions around the Indian Ocean. Thousands of people fled their homes for higher ground, causing roads to be jammed. But it appeared to be a false alarm.

2008

Mumbai Attack

India underwent a succession of coordinated terrorist attacks on November 26, 2008 in Mumbai which continued for four days. No less than 308 people were injured and 174 innocent people died during the attack, 28 being foreigners.

Mumbai's largest train stations, hospitals, five-star hotels, a movie theater and a Jewish center were the targeted areas.

Allegedly, it was the Pakistani members of the Islamic radical organization, Lashkar-e-Taiba, that performed the attack.

A British citizen named Alex Chamberlain, who was dining at one of Mumbai's lavish Hotel, The Oberoi, at the time said to Sky News television that the gunmen were *"talking about British and Americans specifically... there was an Italian guy, who, you know, they said, 'Where are you from?' and he said he's from Italy, and they said, 'Fine,' and they left him alone."*

India's political leaders were castigated by the populace for their incompetence in dealing with the situation following the attacks, thus being held partly responsible for it.

CPSIA information can be obtained
at www.ICGtesting.com
Printed in the USA
LVOW13s1938211116
513933LV00028B/1187/P